NING
UTER PROGRAMS
SOFTWARE ENGINEERS

MIRIAM COLEMAN

PowerKiDS
press.

New York

Published in 2016 by The Rosen Publishing Group, Inc.
29 East 21st Street, New York, NY 10010

First Edition

Editor: Caitlin McAneney
Book Design: Katelyn Heinle

Photo Credits: Cover © iStockphoto.com/Yuri Arcurs; cover, pp. 4–5, 7, 9–10, 12–15, 17–18, 20–23, 26, 28–31 (gear vectors) Hunor Olah/Shutterstock.com; p. 5 zeljkodan/Shutterstock.com; p. 6 scyther5/Shutterstock.com; p. 7 Monty Rakusen/ Cultura/Getty Images; p. 9 (main) Spiderstock/E+/Getty Images; p. 9 (inset) https://upload.wikimedia.org/wikipedia/commons/5/58/FortranCardPROJ039.agr.jpg; p. 10 Mclek/Shutterstock.com; p. 11 Dudarev Mikhail/Shutterstock.com; p. 13 Hero Images/Getty Images; p. 15 Nicola Tree/The Image Bank/Getty Images; p. 17 (top) https://upload.wikimedia.org/wikipedia/commons/a/aa/Margaret_Hamilton_in_action.jpg; p. 17 (bottom) Everett Historical/Shutterstock.com; p. 19 (main) Ann E. Yow-Dyson/Archive Photos/Getty Images; p. 19 (inset) pio3/Shutterstock.com; p. 21 Rob Marmion/Shutterstock.com; p. 23 (top) ullstein bild/Getty Images; p. 23 (bottom) https://upload.wikimedia.org/wikipedia/commons/7/7b/Google_Glass_photo.JPG; p. 24 SpeedKingz/Shutterstock.com; p. 25 https://upload.wikimedia.org/wikipedia/commons/f/fb/Scratch_2.0_Screen_Hello_World.png; p. 27 Klaus Vedfelt/Iconica/Getty Images; p. 29 Dragon Images/Shutterstock.com.

Cataloging-in-Publication Data

Coleman, Miriam.
Designing computer programs: software engineers / by Miriam Coleman.
p. cm. — (Engineers rule!)
Includes index.
ISBN 978-1-5081-4544-8 (pbk.)
ISBN 978-1-5081-4545-5 (6-pack)
ISBN 978-1-5081-4546-2 (library binding)
1. Computer programming — Juvenile literature. I. Coleman, Miriam. II. Title.
QA76.52 C58 2016
001.64′2—d23

Manufactured in the United States of America

CPSIA Compliance Information: Batch #BW16PK: For Further Information contact Rosen Publishing, New York, New York at 1-800-237-9932

CONTENTS

SOFTWARE BEHIND THE SCENES

So much of our lives today depend on computer systems, from banking to health care to communicating with friends and family. All these systems depend on an invisible but necessary side of **technology** called software.

We rarely notice when software works properly, because that's when machines behave the way we expect them to. Our phones make calls, our computers play the videos we want to watch, and our banks keep track of our money. However, when software fails, nothing works, and disaster can strike. Banks can lose money, traffic signals can cause crashes, and computers can go haywire. Software engineers are the people who design, develop, and maintain the programs that work behind the scenes to make sure technology does its job.

Software engineers help the modern world run smoothly.

WHAT IS SOFTWARE?

Software is the name for the instructions and information that a computer needs to do its job. There are two main types of software. Systems software is the information that the computer itself runs on, including the operating system. Applications software is the programs people use to do tasks, such as word processors, web browsers, and video games. The people who create software are sometimes called developers, programmers, or coders.

CODING

The other side of computer technology is hardware. Hardware refers to physical machines, or the parts of computers you can touch. This includes monitors, keyboards, **central processing units**, and printers. Software tells the different types of hardware how to work together.

People use different software for different kinds of jobs. Some software helps keep track of data, or information, while other software can create graphs based on data.

FROM LABORATORIES TO DESKTOPS

Computing devices were first invented to help people perform mathematical calculations in the 19th century. In 1834, Charles Babbage invented the Analytical Engine, which is considered the first mechanical computer. Ada Lovelace, who's considered the first computer programmer, described an **algorithm** that could calculate a series of numbers using the Analytical Engine. It was developed to make the machine do a certain task, and today, that's called software.

Americans John Vincent Atanasoff and Clifford Berry designed and built the first electronic digital computer between 1939 and 1942 at Iowa State University. Early computers weren't something ordinary people could have in their home. They weighed hundreds of pounds and took up an entire room. They were mostly used in science laboratories and, later, by universities and large companies.

The first desktop computers, also known as microcomputers, appeared in the 1970s. Their uses began to expand to include tasks such as communications and word processing. As the use of computers grew, so did the demands for more software—and more software engineers.

PUNCH CARDS

From the days of the earliest computers until the mid-1970s, programs were on paper cards with holes punched in them. Programmers would enter information into the cards by hand using a key punch machine to poke holes that represented either numbers or letters. Each card described one instruction in the program. The punched cards would be fed into a sorting machine, which read the programs and transferred the data to the computer.

PUNCH CARD

Although computers may seem smart, they can only do exactly what they're told. Therefore, the programmer's job is to write down every task in a series of tiny, basic steps. If you forget any of the steps, the program won't work properly.

If you want to tell a computer what to do, you have to know how to communicate with it. Computers don't understand English; they must receive their instructions in a special "machine language." Programming languages are a way to write instructions for the computer in a form humans can better understand. Also known as code, instructions in programming language must be run through a type of software called a compiler to turn it into machine language. Commonly used programming languages include Java, Python, C, and Ruby.

JAVA

Even a task as simple as typing a single letter involves many separate operations that must all be included in the software instructions.

WHAT MAKES IT ENGINEERING?

What makes software engineering stand apart from ordinary computer programming? Engineering, at its heart, is the use of science and math to solve problems. This involves carefully **analyzing** a problem, planning a solution, and examining the results to build safe, **efficient** systems and structures. Civil engineers build roads and highways, and electrical engineers build electrical systems. Meanwhile, software engineers use the principles of traditional engineering to build and maintain reliable, efficient computer software.

Another important aspect of software engineering is project management. This means carefully organizing work among different people and teams in order to meet goals within a set time frame and budget. Because technology changes at such a fast pace, software engineers must be able to release software projects quickly while responding to the needs of their buyers and **clients**.

Like all engineers, software engineers must be aware of what technology is currently available and what's needed to improve and advance today's technology. Software engineers are always looking to the future!

Software engineering involves three main stages. In the first, which is called the definition stage, developers study the problem the project must solve and define what the software needs to do. The second stage is called **implementation**. At this point, developers design how the software will be made, including what its different parts are and how the different parts work together. Once the design is made, they code the different parts, writing out the computer's instructions for each step. Once the project is coded, the developers test out the software to make sure all the parts work and the software does its job.

The final stage is called maintenance. During this stage, developers fix errors in the code and make changes in the software to fit new needs.

As changes are made in the maintenance stage, the software must be tested again to make sure everything still works properly.

SOFTWARE TAKES US TO THE MOON

The first person to coin the term "software engineering" was a NASA scientist named Margaret Hamilton. She worked at a time when the techniques for developing software were not keeping up with increasing needs. People hoped that using the principles of engineering could help manage complex new projects.

Margaret Hamilton was a mathematician and computer scientist who had taught herself computer programming. She became director of the Software Engineering Division of the Massachusetts Institute of Technology Instrumentation Laboratory. This institution was responsible for developing computers for NASA's space missions. In 1969, Hamilton programmed the computer and developed the flight software that allowed the *Apollo 11* astronauts to land safely on the moon.

> Hamilton's software was remarkable because the *Apollo 11*'s computer had to perform many tasks with little memory. In 1986, the Association for Women in Computing rewarded Margaret Hamilton for her extraordinary skill with the Augusta Ada Lovelace Award.

MARGARET HAMILTON

APOLLO 11
LUNAR MODULE

THE MAKING OF MICROSOFT

The world's biggest software company began in 1975, when two college dropouts founded the Microsoft Corporation out of a garage. Bill Gates and Paul Allen had developed a software program using the programming language BASIC for an early microcomputer called the Altair 8800. They helped the Altair's company grow by developing Altair Basic. Microsoft also developed software for Apple and IBM.

Microsoft became famous with the release of a program called Windows in 1985. Windows is an operating system, which is the software that supports the basic functions of a computer. Unlike earlier PC operating systems, which appeared as lines of text on a screen, Windows displayed **graphics**, which users controlled with a mouse. In 1989, Microsoft introduced Microsoft Office, a bundle of software including a word processor and spreadsheet program, which is still popular today.

THE GATES FOUNDATION

Bill Gates's software company has made him one of the richest people in the world. As of 2015, his net worth was over $79 billion. Over time, he felt it was his duty to use his wealth for the common good. In 2000, Gates and his wife Melinda donated $28 billion to found the Bill and Melinda Gates Foundation, which works to improve health care and reduce poverty around the world. In 2008, Gates went from full-time to part-time work at Microsoft to spend more time working with his foundation.

PAUL ALLEN

BILL GATES

Many computer manufacturers include Microsoft Windows and Office when they sell hardware. This helped Microsoft become the leading software manufacturer in the world.

INVENTING THE WORLD WIDE WEB

Software engineering—and the world at large—changed forever in 1989 with the invention of the World Wide Web. Scientists at the European Organization for Nuclear Research were trying to figure out how best to **coordinate** huge, complex scientific projects that many people were working on. A computer scientist named Tim Berners-Lee invented a system where pages of text were connected to each other by "hyperlinks" over a **network** of computers called the Internet. This allowed users to jump from one document to another by clicking on a word or phrase.

Several years later, a new type of software called web browsers brought video, sound, and **animation** into the mix. This made the web more popular among ordinary people and led the way to new technologies and new software demands.

> Today, we use the Internet for just about everything. It makes looking up information fast and easy. The Internet wouldn't be possible without software engineers.

By 1998, finding useful information among the millions of pages on the Internet was a real problem. Two Stanford University computer science students, Sergey Brin and Larry Page, created a search engine, or a type of software that finds and sorts web pages, to solve this. Unlike other search engines, theirs sorted web pages based on the most popular, thus directing users to the most helpful pages. They called it Google.

Google was so successful that they went on to create other programs, including their popular e-mail system, Gmail. Google Maps can give you directions to find your way around countries across the world, while Google Earth provides photos of Earth's surface taken by satellites in space. Google Drive allows users to store files online.

Google Glass is a pair of glasses with a tiny screen that can give you information you ask for just by speaking! It's proof that software can control anything from huge space shuttles to a small pair of glasses.

SERGEY BRIN

Google

LARRY PAGE

BECOMING A SOFTWARE ENGINEER

Software engineers need a strong background in both math and computer science in order to succeed in their field. They also must have excellent problem-solving skills. Most employers seek software engineers with at least a bachelor's degree in a related field. The degree might be in computer science or a more specialized degree in software engineering. Students can also gain more experience training with companies as **interns**.

You can learn to code even before you go to high school and college! There are many coding classes geared towards younger students. Programs such as Scratch and Hopscotch are free and fun.

If you would like to become a software engineer one day, take as many math and science classes as possible before entering college. It's also helpful to get a head start learning the tools of the trade, such as programming languages. You can learn to code with many beginner's programs, such as Scratch and Hopscotch.

SCRATCH

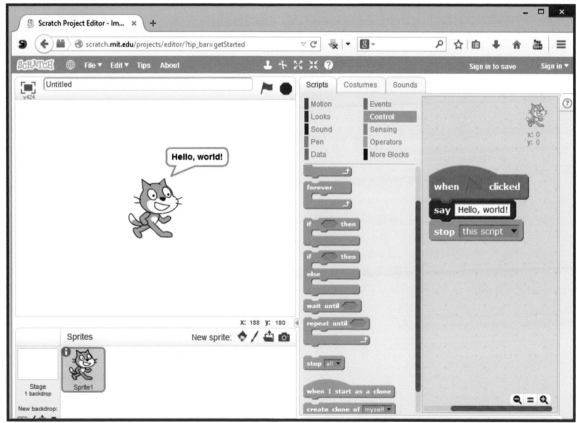

SOFTWARE ENGINEERING CAREERS

Opportunities in software engineering are growing quickly as computer technology continues to advance and become a major part of our everyday lives. There are several different types of jobs in this field.

Computer applications software engineers design, build, and maintain applications. These can take many different forms, including video games, animation software, and systems for businesses to sell products online. Some software engineers create mobile applications for cell phones that keep people informed about news, weather, or government activities.

Computer systems software engineers help companies, educational institutions, and governments set up and maintain their computer systems, including the communications networks that allow employees to connect with each other. An important part of this job is often making sure the company's data is safe and secure.

WHO HIRES?

While some software engineers are self-employed, most work for companies or institutions. They might be hired by companies that specialize in technology, such as Apple, Google, or Microsoft. There are also many opportunities for software engineers in government agencies, schools, and media companies. In fact, nearly every large business or organization today needs software engineers. Some people invent and sell applications on their own.

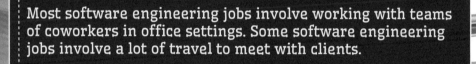

Most software engineering jobs involve working with teams of coworkers in office settings. Some software engineering jobs involve a lot of travel to meet with clients.

THE FUTURE OF SOFTWARE ENGINEERING

Technology has changed so quickly in the 50 years software engineering has been around that it can be hard to imagine what the future may hold. One thing seems certain, though: Software possibilities will only continue to grow.

Many people are talking today about the Internet of Things. This means that an increasing number of objects—from refrigerators to automobiles to traffic lights—will have built-in **sensors** that gather information. These sensors will allow the objects to communicate with other machines and work together using software. For instance, a sensor in your car could use your phone to tell you to get an oil change. As software becomes a part of nearly everything we touch, more and more software engineers will be needed to keep everything running.

Software has the power to make our lives much easier. If you were a software engineer, what kind of application would you create?

SOFTWARE ENGINEERING HISTORY

1834
Charles Babbage invents the Analytical Engine, considered the first mechanical computer.

1843
Ada Lovelace publishes the first computer software.

1884
Herman Hollerith, later the founder of IBM, designs a punch-card system, which is used to add up the numbers from the 1890 U.S. census.

1939–1942
John Vincent Atanasoff and Clifford Berry design and build the first electronic digital computer.

1953
Grace Hopper develops the first computer language, called COBOL.

1975
Bill Gates and Paul Allen found Microsoft.

1976
Steve Jobs and Steve Wozniak found Apple Computer.

1985
Microsoft introduces the Windows operating system.

1989
Tim Berners-Lee invents the World Wide Web.

1998
Sergey Brin and Larry Page release the Google search engine.

2007
Apple introduces the iPhone, expanding software use in phones.

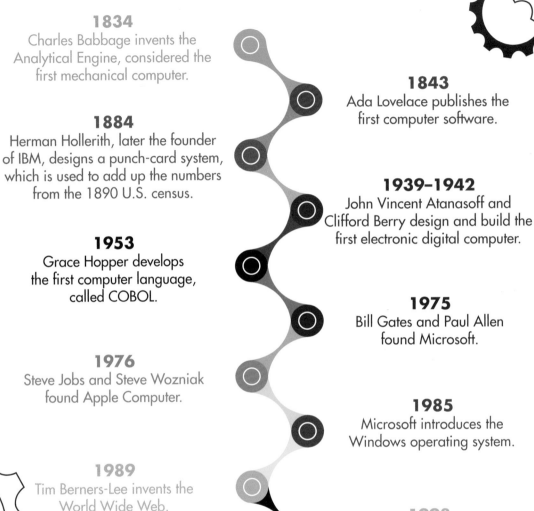

GLOSSARY

algorithm: A set of steps that are followed in order to solve a mathematical problem or complete a computer process.

analyze: To study something deeply.

animation: The technique of making images appear to move.

central processing unit: The part of a computer system that performs the basic operations of the system.

client: Someone who pays a company or other people to do something.

coordinate: To act or work together properly and well.

efficient: Done in the quickest, best way possible.

graphics: Images used to convey information.

implementation: The process of putting a plan into effect.

intern: A student or trainee who works in order to gain experience.

network: A system of computers and other devices that are connected to one another.

sensor: A device that senses heat, light, motion, sound, or smells.

technology: The way people do something using tools and the tools that they use.

INDEX

WEBSITES

Due to the changing nature of Internet links, PowerKids Press has developed an online list of websites related to the subject of this book. This site is updated regularly. Please use this link to access the list: www.powerkidslinks.com/engin/softw